Girls' Night Out

Girls' Night Out

Changing Your Life One Week at a Time

Sandra Robson
with
Ronda Payne and Catherine Anderson

iUniverse, Inc.
New York Lincoln Shanghai

Girls' Night Out
Changing Your Life One Week at a Time

iUniverse books may be ordered through booksellers or by contacting:

iUniverse
2021 Pine Lake Road, Suite 100
Lincoln, NE 68512
www.iuniverse.com
1-800-Authors (1-800-288-4677)

ISBN-13: 978-0-595-37345-1 (pbk)
ISBN-13: 978-0-595-81743-6 (ebk)
ISBN-10: 0-595-37345-3 (pbk)
ISBN-10: 0-595-81743-2 (ebk)

Printed in the United States of America

Contents

JUNE

JULY

AUGUST

SEPTEMBER & OCTOBER

NOVEMBER

DECEMBER

NOTE #1: We save four nights a year for just talking. For saying "What do you need?" Or "What do I do if my son doesn't graduate?" "How do I deal with the ex-husband at the wedding?" Or "Help me, help me, he's driving me crazy!"

NOTE #2: Each of us gets to schedule one pure joy/birthday class a year; something close to her heart or something she always wanted to do.

Introduction

Our great grandmothers were out of luck if they had marital problems or child rearing concerns or feelings of unfulfilled potential. There were no therapy/support groups, no books on how to understand men, no web sites for downloading the latest research. Small wonder those old family albums feature grim-faced women with dull, hopeless eyes.

My Great Aunt Lili was the only older woman I remember who really got a kick out of life. She did it by refusing to get married, by refusing to work more than a couple of hours a day and by moving three thousand miles away from all the relatives who disapproved. Aunt Lili's passion was cowboy movies—the old ones like Roy Rogers and Gene Autry and Hopalong Cassiday and Tom Mix. From them she learned the single, most important lesson in her life and she was happy to share it.

"I said to myself," Aunt Lili would reflect, "where's all the women in them movies? There's lots of men ridin'and shootin'and havin' a bang-up time, but where's the women? And the answer was—there weren't any. The women had all the babies and they worked themself to death. So I said, I'm not doin' that."

Nobody knew how Lili managed financially and of course she had a reputation. But when she came back to the family reunion years later, she was the only older woman who still lit up the room.

Most woman do work today and many of us feel worked to death, overwhelmed by long office hours, households to manage and relationships that need attention. Unlike Aunt Lili, however, cowboy movies aren't our only resource. We are inundated with information on how to make our lives better. If we only had time to read it. If we only had time to act on it. If we only knew <u>how</u> to act on it.

A few years ago two friends and I decided to study a book called *The Artist's Way*. Cathy, Ronda and I met once a week for ten weeks and took turns presenting the chapters and exercises. Sometimes it required delving into past events and relationships and participating in some uncomfortable homework. Like the week we gave up reading and television cold turkey and realized we were addicted to escape mechanisms. But mostly it provided so many surprising, illuminating 'ah-ha's' that we were sorry when we turned the final page. Somewhere in that ten week period our perspectives had shifted significantly. Family worries were less worrisome, we had more energy, problems were easier to deal with, and we laughed a lot more. Even better, our families actually looked forward to our class night. ('Looked forward' translates to: they got their own dinners and found alternate transportation to activities.)

For several weeks we searched unsuccessfully for another book to carry on the lessons and kept our scheduled night inviolate by going to dinner, to movies and shopping. That was fun but it wasn't enough. We missed the challenge, the focus, and the enlightenment of personal growth. Eventually we tackled Dr. Phil's *Life Strategies*, another book with exercises for group study. When that ended, we had shifted perspective still further and learned a number of important things:

<u>First</u>, you can't have personal growth all of the time, you need a break, <u>Second</u>, you can't play all the time, you need a break. <u>Third</u>, learning to balance your life and keeping your inner light bright seems to underlie all growth experiences. <u>Fourth</u>, growing experiences can be scheduled without organizing yourself into oblivion.

The following chapters contain a year's worth of weekly activities for lighting up your life, changing the way you look at the world, and helping you grow. We've done all of them and many more in the last five years but we consider these the best. By sharing our experiences, format and suggestions, we hope you will be inspired to form your own group. We tried to keep our learning sessions balanced between five general categories: Discovery Days, Study Days, Renewal Days, Creative Days, and Entertainment Days. Our intent was loving, steady growth with gentle lessons and considerable laughter, but there is no right or wrong way to learn how to make your life better.

We found the following guidelines helpful:

* Take turns choosing projects, outings and activities. If it's your turn and your mind's blank trade your night with someone else.
* No one is in charge. If you're the dynamic, leader type, who's wonderful at it, learn to follow for awhile without judging somebody else's leadership style. You'll get what you're supposed to get out of it—it just works out that way. If you're the shy, retiring type who hates to lead and avoids it as much as possible, learn to do it without criticizing yourself. You grow most when you contribute.
* Keep the class a workable size. Too many people involved in the group leads to scheduling problems and no-shows. When members don't show up, it changes the dynamic. Also, too-large classes make it hard for everyone to contribute. We found three ideal.
* Schedule one two-to-three hour class a week (or every other week) and stick to the same day. Change it only in an emergency. If Tuesday night class is on your calendar, you won't double book yourself accidentally. You're committed to you.
* Make sure class doesn't become a non-ending therapy session, i.e., one person discusses personal problems all night long. If someone has a problem and

she wants to talk, take twenty minutes and really listen. Listening helps and the problem doesn't have to get solved. If significantly more time than that is needed, get some private therapy.

* Be sure you trust the people in your group. Opportunities for growth involve experiences that are uncomfortable as well as joyful and you will probably want to share some of them.

So, find two or three friends, set a meeting time, and work and play along with us, expanding your joy factor, your creative vision, and lighting up the rooms you enter in the best Aunt Lily fashion. She found her own way all by herself (with a little help from Hopalong Cassidy). We need, value, and appreciate the help of our girlfriends. After all, your partner may be the best thing that ever happened to you, but there's no way he's going to make you little crust-less sandwiches wrapped in colored foil and ribbons when you're having a bad day.

Oh, one more thing…Be Prepared for Change. When you work in a group with the intent to improve your life, mental and physical shifts occur. You may lose weight, switch jobs, move house, and reevaluate relationships. *Don't let the thought of change stop or slow your forward movement.* Personal growth is not about trading in the things and people you love for better specimens. It's about *you*. About you becoming kinder, more loving and more approving of yourself and others. About keeping your own personal light bright instead of trying to brighten the lights of everyone else. And about understanding what lights up your world.

> "Cheers to a new year and another chance to get it right."
> Oprah Winfrey, O Magazine.

January   Week 1   Renewal

Every year, first week in January, we start over, fresh, clean-slate, brand new; clearing away beliefs that no longer work for us, sweeping out the clutter of negative thoughts that have accumulated over the last twelve months, making room for the things we want in our lives.

Since we live in Florida, this is how we do it. We meet at the beach around three in the afternoon. No matter how cold it is, and it's often cold in January, we show up prepared to swim, which means bathing suits layered under jeans and sweaters. We bring these things:

slips of paper	bottle of olive oil
black magic markers	beach blanket
cigarette lighter	towels
round cake pan	

We find a good place to put down the blanket—out of the wind if possible though it usually isn't—and sit cross-legged in a circle. Then we take a few minutes to think of people we need to forgive, people we need to ask to forgive us, and to list grudges, resentments or fears we've been holding onto lately. We write these on slips of paper and fold them up tightly. Then we take turns burning them in the cake pan, saying after each one, 'I release you and I let you go.'

When all the slips of paper have been reduced to ash, we toss the pan and let the wind whip the rest of it away. Then we sit for awhile and let our minds clear. If someone wants to say something, she says it, but often we simply sit in silence and let the combination of wind and waves carry away the feelings we've released, leaving in their place a sense of lightness, calm, and order.

Now for the fun, and brave, part. We strip down to our bathing suits and prepare to go in the water. And since we're not members of the Polar Bear Club, (Florida does <u>too</u> get cold in the winter) we rub olive oil on our arms and legs and rub sand over that. That does two things. It warms you up a little for the projected dip and it let you scrub away negative or cluttered thoughts that may be clinging to you. It's kind of like the Dead Sea Salt Scrub treatment at the spa only eighty dollars cheaper. If the oil and sand are a little too weird for you, you can skip that part, but there's nothing like running into the ocean and back out again in the middle of January—a minute and a half is our top time—feeling mentally and physically energized and ready to start the new year.

Afterwards, wet, shivering and giggling, we change from freezing suits to warm clothes in the nearest bathroom, do the best we can with our hair, and head to the tiki bar for a glass of wine.

There are lots of ways to have clearing ceremonies. We're lucky enough to live near the beach and we like having the inspiration of an entire ocean, but ceremony is more important than site. Releasing beliefs and attitudes that are no longer useful and making space for those that are, can be easily accomplished at your own kitchen table. Just keep an eye on the smoke alarm if it's been a traumatic year.

> "I'm a woman. I'm used to doing a lot of things
> I don't want to." Sharon Stone in Catwoman

January   Week 2   Personal Taste

This is a tricky lesson because many women don't really know what they like. At a workshop I once gave, participants were asked to make a list of ten things they enjoyed doing and ten things they wanted out of life. Out of sixty women, fifty-four realized they'd made a list of things their mates or children or friends or parents enjoyed/wanted and had to start over. So ask yourself, do you really love bowling with your husband three times a week? If so, great. If not, why do you do it so often?

It's important to figure out what it is you really enjoy but don't ask your nearest and dearest to enlighten you. They may know, but the question is, why don't you?

To find out, start with some basic, easy choices. People rarely fool themselves about what they like to smell. Something either smells good or it doesn't, no matter what the guys down at the fish market tell you.

List 4 things that smell good to you   _____
                                        _____
                                        _____
                                        _____

List 2 things you don't like to smell: _____
                                        _____

Now compare your lists with each other. Look for similarities and differences.

Touch is another sense that's easy to determine. Do you like the feel of silk, velvet, an emery board, grease, dirt, hot soapy dishwater, expensive hand cream? Tickling, tingling, pins and needles, having the cold creeps?

List three things that feel good to the touch: _____
                                               _____
                                               _____

List two things you don't like to touch: _____
                                               _____

Share your answers. Are your choices radically different from those of your friends?

Now move on to taste, which gets a little more difficult. The food channel chef tells you ginger duck has an amazing depth of flavor you won't want to miss. Your Cousin Margery insists her award winning potato salad is mouth watering and disappears immediately at potluck dinners. So, do you really like the taste of duck? Do you like award winning potato salad? Or is it just that you should if you're the right sort of person?

List three things you absolutely love to taste: _____
                                                _____
                                                _____

Now list 3 things you always wanted to like, but honestly never have.
_____
_____

Having trouble on the last one? Check the examples below from our group:

1. Martini. Clear, crystal liquid, elegantly shaped glass, big fat olives, twists of lemon. A beautiful, sophisticated drink for the person I always wanted to be. But the truth is, I detest martinis, particularly those made with gin.
2. Black licorice. The other kids obviously loved it, traded it, gave you some if you were their friend. So I ate those nasty, chewy black ropes for years and smiled my thanks. The truth? Almost made me throw up.
3. That damned award winning potato salad. To me, it was huge chunks of potato swimming in mayonnaise and bland, bland, bland, but I ate it throughout my formative years. And I wasn't even in the will.

If you've been counting, you know you've got two senses left—sight and hearing. And that's where individual taste gets complicated. Vision and hearing are our two major learning modes. It's easy to get sensory overload from all the colors and shapes and sounds and rhythms of the remarkable world we inhabit. And that's if you're paying attention.

Take hearing for instance. Do you like the sound of rain, thunder, the neighbor's band saw, motorcycles, wind blowing the sable palms? Do you hear different kinds of silence? Do you notice voices when people speak? The deep, soothing tone of the radio announcer, the shrill woman in line at the grocery store, the auctioneer rattling off unintelligible bids, the kid with a voice like a bullfrog? Do you listen to the texture of their voices as well as the messages? Can you repeat messages back without writing them down? What music do you really like: Mozart, Billy Joel, Kid Rock?

Write down some songs, bands, tapes or CD's that you like listening to when you're the only one around. Star the ones you love.

_____   _____
_____   _____

Which ones don't you love? If it depresses you to hear Tschaikovsky's Symphony #6, say so. It depressed him too. He cried all the way to Paris while he was composing it.

Some music I don't like is: _____
_____

Last, and hardest, let's look at vision. (No pun intended). Before you can choose what you like, you have to see what's really out there.

Most people aren't good observers. I learned that years ago in a college art class. The instructor brought in a crate of naval oranges and told everybody to choose one and study it for five minutes. I remember looking at mine for maybe ten seconds with a feeling halfway between boredom and scorn. After all, it was round and orange, right? How hard was that? We returned the oranges to the crate, went back to our seats and were told to take out charcoal pencils and drawing tablet, which we did. Ho-hum. And then she instructed us to go back to the table and find the orange we'd studied for five minutes.

No one was successful. We spent ten futile minutes manhandling the fruit, frantically studying the actual shape, pebbly texture, stem marks, etc. Eventually she called a halt and we did the exercise over. I was relieved and gratified when I recognized the wavy error in the grocer's mark and was able to reclaim my very own orange. From then on, when the lady said 'look,' I looked.

Even when you're a good observer, there are so many choices of color and fabric and content in art, fashion, and design, so many opinions from experts and would-be experts, that it may be hard to pinpoint your personal style. Do you like celery green sweaters or are they just in the window this year? Is your den painted cranberry marsh red because it makes you feel warm inside or because the decorator loves it? Do you long for a purple car but drive a beige one? Is everything in your house and closet white, black and taupe because those are easy colors to work with or do you really love minimalism?

List three colorful items you've always wanted and still don't have:

_____
_____
_____

List three items you live with and don't like:

_____
_____
_____

Once you begin to get clear on your personal taste, move on to activities. What do you truly like to do? If you had one full day all to yourself, with unlimited time and money, how would you spend it?

Playing tennis
Eating at a new Thai restaurant
Water skiing
Singing torch songs in a nightclub
At the Renoir exhibit
In bed, ordering in pizza, and watching the soaps
Walking the beach—any beach
Trying on designer dresses
Painting a picture
Taking a cooking lesson
Shopping for new towels and sheets
Getting a facial and new hairstyle
Dancing to Sixties songs at a retro club
Curling up in a rocker on the porch with a good mystery
Taking your husband and a picnic to the park
Taking your boyfriend and a picnic to the park
Taking them both to the park and forgetting the picnic
    (Just wanted to see if you were paying attention)

Describe your perfect day: _____

_____

If you were going to plan a vacation all by yourself, where would you go?

_____

Where in the entire world would you like to live? _____

_____

What kind of books do you enjoy reading? _____

_____

What movies are your favorites? _____

_____

Now list some things that you don't like and be honest. If you dislike New Year's Eve because it always seems a night of unrealistic expectations, or clowns because they've given you the creeps since you were little, or reading Proust though intellectuals rave about him, or Victoria's Secret underwear which everyone knows is the ultimate expression of femininity, say so. It's your style, not somebody else's that matters. If you're not honest about what you like, you will never recognize it when you see it.

Some things I've never liked but always thought I should are:

_____

_____

_____

Question: Once you've identified the things you truly love, are you going to do only those things from this moment forward in a great burst of personal freedom?

Absolutely not. It's not fair to your significant others to suddenly change the rules just because you've had a revelation. You wouldn't like it if your partner decided his only love was golf and he played it seven days a week and made everybody else do it too.

What you will do is begin to integrate some of the things you love into your regular routine, continue to clarify your likes and dislikes, spend time exploring and learning new things, and be grateful you live in a time and place where you're free to have choices and act on them.

"Between living and dreaming there is a third thing. Guess it." Antonio Machado

January   Week 3   Portable Treasure Maps

Treasure mapping has been around for years and there are lots of ways to do it. When you make a treasure map, you always show yourself in the desired situation as if it had already happened. It's sort of a visual fake it til you make it. My initial effort was an ink drawing taped to the bathroom mirror. It showed me working at a job I really wanted but didn't think I had a chance to land. I looked at it every day and when I actually got the job a few weeks later, I became a true believer. I immediately replaced the map with a picture of Brad Pitt.

Treasure maps can be valuable tools for growth. People I know have used them to improve relationships, attract the right relationship, to grow spiritually, to change jobs, to lose weight, even to get a badly needed computer. When you decide what you really want in life and create a visual picture of it, your energy becomes focused on that goal. You subconsciously align yourself in that direction and become open to opportunities you might have missed or ignored before.

Treasure maps can be any size, from giant poster boards to 3x5 cards. We like small ones that prop up where you can see them and can be moved from place to place easily. Also, it's better to keep your maps simple and specific, one for work, one for relationships, one for health, etc. If you want a lot of things out of life and create a giant collage, mish-mashing them all together, your energy gets scattered.

For a portable treasure map, you will need:

    5x8 index cards
    A pile of your favorite magazines
    Pictures of yourself
    Scissors
    Glue or tape
    Colored markers
    An empty key ring or single notebook ring

You will also need to depict specific goals. Nebulous verbal pictures like 'a good life' 'internal peace' or 'everybody to get along' accompanied by waving hand gestures are unclear and therefore unattainable. First decide precisely what you like and want. Then prepare a clear picture of it by cutting pictures and words from magazines that show you accomplishing your goals or already in the situations you desire. Attach them to the front and back of the note cards and put a picture of your face wherever appropriate. Add words you find inspiring, like **DYNAMIC, SUCCESSFUL, BETTER PAYING JOB, ELEGANT, EXCITING FABULOUS LOVE LIFE** etc. Then punch a hole in one corner of the cards and slide them on the ring. This makes it easy to carry your goals wherever you go.

If cut and paste isn't your thing, you can always draw or paint yourself receiving the Nobel Prize, fitting into a size six, honeymooning with George Clooney, or ballooning across the Alps.

One final thing. Look at your map several times a day. That keeps you focused. If you decide you really don't want something you've pictured, take it off and put something else in its place. You're allowed to change your mind, your life, and your creative vision anytime you want.

"If I ever go looking for my heart's desire again, I won't look further than my own back yard."
Dorothy in the Wizard of Oz.

January   Week 4   Movie Night

Going to the movies isn't as elegant as it once was. There are no ushers in dark suits guiding you to your seat with shaded flashlights, no opulent old movie houses with names like the Palace and the Grand and the Fox, no plush, padded balconies, no maroon velvet curtains rising slowly amid lashings of gold braid. Still, there's nothing better than rolling up to your nearest 18 superplex, arming yourself with a giant buttered popcorn and a soda and settling in for a couple of hours of pure escape.

We have several movie nights a year and we take turns choosing what to see. There aren't any rules but we like films that lift you up, lighten whatever current load you're carrying, and make you feel like dancing all the way home. When we toted up our current favorites, we agreed on these:

Ya Ya Sisterhood	As Good As It Gets
Calendar Girls	My Best Friends' Wedding
Sister Act	Bridgette Jones's Diary
Under the Tuscan Sun	Working Girl
Something's Got to Give	Four Weddings and a Funeral
About a Boy	Shall We Dance

Do you see a pattern? Absolutely. They're about people searching for something they want in life and not realizing they already have it. They're also about another of life's sometimes painful lessons—the need to discard old situations and attitudes to make room for new ones. When it's time to move on, you always have a choice. Either get yourself moving forward or prepare to be moved.

Movies offer true stories, stories you wish were true, stories you hope never come true. They're eye-opening reminders that the life you're living at this moment is the result of what you yourself have created. That if you dislike what you have, it's time to stop blaming other people or circumstances and create something different. As in better. As in heart's desire. You will never have a heart's desire that will not manifest. In fact it will manifest bigger than your vision. All you have to do is open your eyes and look around. Movies, like life, are simply their creator's vision, a big screen, technicolor, personal treasure map. Watching them reminds you that in your personally constructed motion picture, you get to choose the treasure, decide where it will be buried, and make up your mind how quickly you're going to find it.

February   Week 1   Body Exotica

When a local gym advertised a class called Body Exotica as "an exercise in releasing our inhibitions, learning to appreciate our bodies and exploring movements," we pulled on our spandex and went to check it out. As a precautionary measure, we stopped at a nearby cafe for a glass of wine.

The wine helped, but not enough. For the first twenty minutes we giggled uncontrollably from our spot in the very back of the room, even though the instructor had mercifully dimmed the lights. Warm-up exercises included wiggling our hips sideways in figure eights and dropping our heads forward almost to the floor to look back between spread legs. We learned to shake our hair out wildly, shimmy our shoulders, crawl like stalking tigers across the floor, and undulate down to a squat and back up again as if we were enclosed in glass tubes. Then there was pole dancing, strut walking, and a little number called 'the windex' where we stood with our backs against the mirrored walls and slid up and down, arms wafting gracefully above our heads.

The instructor was upbeat and funny but the workout was strenuous. Who knew exotic dancing involved so many stretches, squats and thrusts? Everyone in the class, from young girls to older women worked hard to get the exercises right but the only guy, despite a linebacker build and numerous tattoos, had all the moves. Sometimes we just did what he was doing.

You'd think, when you're so busy concentrating, there'd be no time for judgmental remarks about your own body. Not so. Even with low lighting and dim reflections in the mirrors, we had comments: "When I went to school you got booted out for dancing like this." "The only way I could earn a dollar pole dancing is by selling the poles." "My hips don't roll like that, but then they're about the size of Ohio."

The class lasted an hour but it flew by. When it was all over, we decided: A) We were not as flexible as we had previously thought, B) Next time we'd have two glasses of wine, and C) Our husbands were going to pay very close attention when we explained what we did in class that night.

Body Exotica may not be an offering in your town. If not, check out other exercise classes in the area: kick-boxing, Taekwondo, belly dancing, etc. Discovering a new, exciting activity and trying it on for size not only stretches you physically, but mentally.

"It is not your business to determine how good it (your expression of art) is; not how valuable it is; nor how it compares with others. It is your business to keep it yours....to keep the channel open."
Martha Graham in a letter to Agnes DeMille

February   Week 2   Clay Cafe

Sometimes normal daily creativity—planning a meal, painting a room, sewing up Halloween costumes—just isn't enough. Sometimes you need to create an actual Work of Art, a, soul satisfying, form-doesn't-follow-function masterpiece of inspired color combinations and avante garde shapes. There are lots of options. You can take painting lessons, chisel a block of granite into a giant pointing finger, or get out your colored pencils and talk your partner into posing au naturel. But if you're not quite ready for radical sculpture or surrealist eyeballs or pastel drawings of male nudes, you can do what we did: start with a place like the Clay Cafe.

The Clay Cafe is actually a ceramics shop that seats about twenty-five. You can rent it out for a birthday party or a woman's club get-together or just make a reservation for yourself if you feel like two solo hours of creativity. The owner provides drinks and finger snacks, artistic expertise and shelves of green ware plates, bowls, tiles, platters, teapots, and small sculptures. Your job is to purchase the pieces you like and paint them. When you've finished, the owner fires them for you and displays them in the window until you pick them up.

We made a reservation for three on our regular class night but not all of us were thrilled about it. That's because one of us is severely painting-challenged. And sensitive about it too. So, feeling some comic relief might be called for, that one suggested that as long as we were being artistic, we should dress and act like artists for the class. When nobody jumped on the idea, it became a challenge: "I dare you. Five bucks says you're too embarrassed to do it."

Everybody had varying ideas of how artists really dressed. One of us arrived in black leotards and a beret, one in a beret and smock, and one wore a lacy, gypsy-style skirt, a babushka and dangling bead earrings. Our plan—to park directly in front of the Cafe and dart inside before anybody saw us—didn't work out. There were a lot of people downtown that night and the streets were jammed. The closest parking place was six blocks away and we had to put on our sunglasses, walk fast, and tough it out.

By the time we got to the shop and inside, we had succumbed to Group Glee. Group Glee is a malady prevalent among preschoolers and kindergarteners. It starts when one kid dissolves into hysterical laughter for no apparent reason and the rest are immediately infected. Minimally funny occurrences become fodder for heart-stopping delirium and merely looking at another person can send everybody into spasms. Unchecked, Group Glee can last from fifteen to twenty minutes. That evening we had it for two and a half hours.

We calmed down a little initially as the Cafe's owner offered us sodas or white wine, showed us hundreds of pieces of green ware, and laid out an array of paints, brushes, scrapers and sponges. But as we started working, we got sillier and sillier. There was a large stuffed gorilla perched on a chair in the corner of the shop and we decided he'd make a perfect muse. With the owner's permission, we seated him on a chair next to us and when we found out his name was KoKo we decided we needed names too. Artistic names. One of us wanted to be called KiKi after the famous model in twenties Paris who posed nude for Picasso and other Lost Generation artists. One of us took the name KayKay. Nobody however, wanted to be KooKoo or KahKah. Luckily, we were the only people in the place that night and the owner seemed to think we were amusing rather than seriously disturbed.

At the end of the evening Cathy had painted a large round plate with raised flowers, Ronda a serving platter in the shape of a fish, and I had decorated two tiles. When we picked the pieces up a few days later, two of them had turned out beautifully. Ronda's platter was a mélange of jewel colored scales: cobalt blue, turquoise, orange and pale yellow. Cathy's plate was sponge painted in peach and pale blue rose blossoms with gold stars around the rim. However, my tiles looked like something emerging men did on cave walls in the dark. After trying to fob them off on my mother, an old friend, and Goodwill, I finally put them on my counter top and sat hot things on them, hoping they would break. No such luck. Your art, fragile as it is, is still your art. And the medium you choose to explore it is up to you.

"We are the products of editing, rather than authorship." George Wald

February   Week 3   Makeover Night

We love this class and redo it periodically, not just for the glamorous lift it gives us but for the belly laughs. It's a three stage lesson.

First, arrange for one of the make-up counters at a local department store to take all of you at a specific time. They'll probably make you up one at a time, but that's fine, the others will watch and comment. That's right, comment.

Throw away all ideas about how you usually look or should look and trust the girl who's doing the make-up to choose the colors, and shades that suit you best. This is definitely a two-edged sword if you get someone with no taste or training—but hey, it's supposed to be fun and the worst that can happen is you won't like the end product and will have to scrub it off in the mall bathroom with a couple of tissues. This will still result in a healthy glow.

If one of the new colors or treatments works for you and you love it, buy it and *use* it. Make-up specialists say make-up looks change every six months. That's a little speedy for the three of us, but there's no point in looking like nineteen seventy-eight either. The idea is, see what's new, see if you like it, and make a small, or large, change in your appearance. A new look will make you glow for a couple of weeks but even if you purchase nothing, just wallowing for an hour in glossy lip colors, the new blushers, and flaw-concealing powders is luxurious and soul satisfying.

Second, take your newly made up face and a throwaway camera up the escalator and look at clothes. What you wear is important because of the messages it sends to people you meet. Messages like: 'I'm the best candidate for this job,' "My iron's broken," "I am not high on my personal priority list," or "I dressed in the dark this morning."

Your assignment is to put together three outfits, one for evening, one for work, and one for casual wear. However, there's a catch. You're not going to choose. Your friends will choose for you. They'll pick colors and styles that they think look good on you and you'll do the same for them. You will not say: A. 'I never

16

wear brown', B. 'It's too clingy. My gut sticks out' or C. 'I couldn't possibly wear that without a jacket or sweater or trench coat or tent.'

Just put on what you're given, smile your most seductive, professional, or casual smile, and say Cheese. Be sure to take pictures of every outfit. If you love any of the clothes, and your budget allows, buy and wear them. Something new and different that flatters you will lift your spirits far longer than an extra large bag of chocolate chips.

Third, when your pictures have been developed, put them on the refrigerator or the bulletin board or the dashboard of your car, and enjoy them. When your husband asks what you learned in class that night, tell him you're learning to appreciate potential you never knew you had.

February   Week 4   Japanese Dinner

When it's your turn for Pure Joy Night, you're allowed to keep the activity a secret
and that's what Cathy did. She picked us up and drove to a small shopping plaza
a few miles away. Ronda and I scanned the storefronts, looking for a clue to the
night's activity. Irish Pub? Possibly. Real estate office? Probably not. Hairdresser?
Maybe. Maybe we were getting a makeover to revive us. It had been a particularly
frazzling day; busses running late, solid rain most of the morning, a student who
bit two teachers and ran outside into a road full of traffic, a crushed package of
cheese doodles for lunch. Anything short of mud wrestling was going to be an
improvement.

We were still trying to figure it out as we walked past the pub, the offices and
the salon, turned the corner and entered a door flanked by white herons winging
their way across a cerulean blue screen. Cathy's surprise was a Japanese restaurant.

The dining room was small but the dozen or so rattan tables were separated
from each other by cream colored screens and small potted trees. Any of the
secluded dining areas would have suited us but the hostess ignored them and led
us to a booth built on a raised platform with a long low table and slightly lower
pillowed benches. Two sides of the booth were lined with rice paper panels and
straw matting and the third was a window looking out over a tiny patio and fountain. The table was set with blue and gold dragon plates and chopsticks resting
gracefully on matching stands. We had barely kicked off our shoes and settled in
when a girl arrived with a wicker basket of hot wet cloths and glasses of plum
wine. We wiped our hands, sipped wine and the food began to arrive in courses.
Fresh sliced cucumber and daikon (white radish) with wasabi sauce, sushi spider
rolls with crab, miso soup. A cedar tray with appetizers—'something from the
ocean (scallops) and something from the mountains (beef)' the girl told us—a
bamboo basket of tempura shrimp and vegetables with a gingery sauce, mochi
(grilled rice cakes), pork wrapped asparagus rolls, grilled squid. We ate it all, no
matter what it was called or how wildly different it looked from a burger and

fries. The combination of spicy, salty, sour and sweet flavors, the elegant presentation, and the serene atmosphere made it a satisfying, luxurious meal. Cathy had not only reserved the special table, she had pre-ordered all the dishes so we didn't have to ask questions, make choices, or even think. It was pure heaven and we zenned right out.

By the time we were served green tea in ceramic cups, the restaurant had filled with people but it still had the feeling of a snug harbor tucked away in a rackety world. Babies didn't cry, children didn't crawl under the tables, voices weren't raised, no-one knocked over a wineglass.

It was better than two hours of therapy. After a long, less than fruitful day at work, nothing beats taking off your shoes and being waited on hand and bare foot.

"The spirit of self-help is the root of all genuine growth in the individual. Help from without is often enfeebling in its effects, but help from within invariably invigorates."
Samuel Smiles, 1859.

March/April   Weeks 1-8   Study Nights

Self help books come in all sizes, shapes, and thicknesses. Some tell you how to eradicate bad habits, fear, anxiety, depression, low self-esteem, stress, phobias, and bad men in your life. Others want to help you dress better, eat better, decorate better, get along with your boss and attract your perfect mate.

We've studied a lot of them over the years. Some are excellent tools for helping you strip away the behaviors that keep you from being who you really are. Some are merely boring. We usually choose the workbook/exercise types because they don't overwhelm you with pages and pages of eye glazing print, and because you're more likely to retain and use what you learn if you stop to think, write and share information as you go along. Sometimes you 'get it' just by listening to other people's experiences.

Some of our favorite workbook-style activity books are:

Dr. Phil's Life Strategies—Dr. Phil McGraw
The Artist's Way—Julia Cameron
You Can Heal Your Life, the Companion Book—Louise Hay
Who Are You? 101 Ways of Seeing Yourself—Malcolm Godwin

Other books that we simply read and discussed were:

The Four Agreements—Don Miguel Ruiz
The Seat of the Soul—Gary Zukov
Simple Abundance—Sara Ban Breathnach
Feel the Fear and Do It Anyway—Susan Jeffers

Don't Sweat the Small Stuff—Richard Carlson
Snap Out of It—Herbert Cohen

Take turns choosing books that work for you and once chosen, see them through to the end. We created an eight week format for ourselves because we liked the idea of a two month personal journey but there are other options. You may want to divide a book into two four week sections or design even shorter study periods interspersed with activities. Whatever you decide, pay close attention to passages or chapters that make you feel uncomfortable or resentful or resistant. Sometimes your next major breakthrough is only one tiny objectionable paragraph away.

There is no love sincerer than the love of
food." George Bernard Shaw.

May   Week 1   Cooking Greek

Eating at a real Greek restaurant is my idea of heaven. I love the bowls of cured
olives on the tables, the whitewashed walls, the family members laughing and eating at a round table in the corner, the balalaika music. Just reading the menu
brings back memories of an unforgettable ferry trip through the Greek Islands.
The harbor at Symi with its deep blue water, sun bleached houses, fishing boats
tied to the jetty and platters of freshly fried calamari. The taverna in Rhodes
where we learned an old Greek dance called The Drunken Man and wolfed down
dolmas and taramosalata and stifado. The donkey ride up a steep pebbled path to
the Acropolis at Lindos with our picnic lunch of spankopita. The Monastery of
Panormitis where we lit tall thin white candles in the ancient darkness of the
katholikon, then returned to the outside world and a nearby cafe for wine and
moussaka.

Unfortunately, those memories aren't revived very often. There are no Greek
restaurants in our immediate area and although I learned to cook my favorite
dishes several years ago, my husband isn't a big fan of either Greek food or large
amounts of garlic. So every once in a while, when it's my turn to plan class, I
organize a Greek feast.

Sometimes we just have wine and an appetizer platter filled with dolmas
(grape leaves stuffed with a combination of ground beef, rice, and spices), fried
eggplant strips with skordalia (a thick garlic sauce made with bread or potatoes)
or pita bread spread with taramosalata (a dip made with carp roe caviar and bread
and olive oil). Sometimes we have moussaka (eggplant and meat casserole),
spanokopitta (spinach feta pie), or stifado (a beef stew cooked with wine).

Whatever the dish, for awhile I revisit a country whose food is as rich,
earthy, and tantalizing as its literature and history. And I remember that way
back in A.D. 200, when many people still considered raw meat the daily special, a Greek scholar named Athenaeus penned *The Philosophy of Dining*, the
world's first cookbook.

Most of us have indelible food memories—the lamb birthday cakes covered in white coconut that your great aunt used to make, pina colada pancakes at that cozy bed and breakfast in Seattle, cous cous and cardomom tea at a tiny North African cafe in Paris.

What was your most perfect meal? If you like to cook, reproduce it and invite your friends to share the memory. If basting and poaching isn't your thing, take a cooking lesson, hire a chef or find a restaurant that specializes in your own special comfort food. And eat up; it's good for your soul.

May   Week 2   Spa Nights

Spa visits are a luxurious way to cosset and spoil yourself when life isn't living up to its build up. We've had three, widely divergent spa experiences. The first was like checking into a luxury hotel. We were assigned private lockers, thick terry bathrobes and given a tour of the amenities. Then we changed into bathing suits and headed for the outdoor mineral pools. After soaking in the dead sea salt pool, the French salt pool, and a small bubbling pool shaded by white roman columns, bougainvillea and palm trees, we went back inside to try out the cedar wood sauna, the steam room and the Jacuzzi. By then we were totally relaxed and ready for naps, but it was time for facials so we slipped into robes and slippers and pattered to the waiting room. There, overstuffed chairs, herbal teas, platters of fresh papaya and kiwi slices, and the latest women's magazines kept us occupied until our technicians came to collect us.

Our facials were lavish—right down to the heated mitts that kept your hands warm while your face was being cleansed, toned, scrubbed and moisturized. Everything was perfection. The only hard thing was staying awake and alert enough to drive back home.

We weren't as lucky with our second spa experience. This one was at a startup day spa in a strip mall which advertised a series of three reduced-price facials and was apparently operating on an extremely thin shoestring. It did not live up to its name of Nearly Heaven. We arrived for simultaneously scheduled treatments and were taken one by one over a period of two and a half hours.

The facials here were abbreviated and the woman in white scrubs who gave them, kept reminding us that if we'd paid the full price we'd be getting a lot more attention. The treatment room was a white walled, 8x10 square with a massage table in the center, dim lighting, and no window. It did have a pretend window however, a blue curtain attached to one wall over a hand-painted tree. The woman popped a tape in a boom box to provide serenity and relaxation but since it kept getting jammed, it was irritating rather than restful. There appeared to be no running water in the room and the cleansing cloths used on your face were rinsed out in a crock pot. At no time was the technician observed changing the water in the pot.

The massage was slightly better but it was given by an ex-Realtor who had yet to receive his LMT license. None of us left feeling pampered but we did get the giggles on the way to the car so it wasn't a wasted evening.

Our third spa experience was a disaster which involved price gouging, false advertising, and indifferent personnel. This one was only funny several months later.

There's nothing more energizing than a soothing spa visit. Consider it a gift to yourself and research it carefully before you go. Then, leave all your troubles at the check-in counter, and prepare to be pampered.

"Don't die with your music still in you." Wayne Dyer

May   Week 3   Diva Night

All my life I wanted to be a torch singer. Unfortunately I had absolutely no singing ability at all. I learned that when I tried out for junior high chorus and the music teacher looked like somebody was standing on her neck. She did let me join, but she suggested I should sing very softly or maybe just move my lips. It didn't matter what she said because in my daydreams I was wearing a long, low-cut fabulous dress and blasting Cry Me a River to the back of the house. My voice was breathy, husky, better than Barbra Streisand, Lena Horne and Judy Garland combined, and when the last poignant note died in the smoky air, club patrons stumbled to their feet in stunned applause.

Realizing daydreams doesn't have to require great infusions of cash, although it helps. (For example, the lottery winner who rented out Boston Gardens for the day and pretended to be one of the Celtics or the woman who bought a tiny French village because she'd always wanted to be queen of something.) With a little preparation and a little help from my friends, I got to experience torch singing firsthand.

We started with a singing lesson from our friend Jane, a gifted vocalist and music teacher. She taught us to breathe from the diaphragm instead of shallowly from our lungs and ran us through a series of complicated exercises. We panted like puppies, went up and down the scales several times, and practiced singing a kind of aaaoooh'O' while pretending to have ping pong balls in our mouths. And Jane told us, bless her heart, that some people are born American Idols and some aren't but the ones who aren't can improve by limbering up their dormant singing muscles. By the end of the practice we were singing in our proper ranges, reaching a few of those high notes and ready to move on to Phase Two.

In Phase Two, we changed clothes and got ready to do a solo and a group gig. Both Ronda and I had unworn red dresses, complete with spangles, in the back of our closets (one of them had been hanging there twenty years) and Ronda's mother sent a third dress, an Oleg Cassini original, red sequined, with cleavage, that fit Cathy perfectly. We added strappy shoes, feather boas, flashy earrings, climbed back onto our stools, clicked on the microphones, and cut loose.

Ronda sang Over the Rainbow, and I took a shot at Cry Me a River. Cathy opted out of a solo since her early singing experiences were worse than mine, but the three of us collaborated on several of our favorite songs. We did them over and over again until we got tired, then took pictures, changed back to real clothes and took Jane to a Chinese restaurant where we soothed our vocal cords with jasmine tea, Jade Shrimp and Broccoli Beef.

There's something about singing that makes your heart bigger. Maybe it's merely ancient programming since human beings are believed to have sung before they talked. Maybe it's the tones or the resonance or the frequency. Whatever it is, I learned an important thing. Pretending to be a torch singer was about as good as the real thing. Better maybe, since none of my best and wildest daydreams ever involved performing on the road three hundred nights a year.

If you've never had a desire to be Celine Dion, skip the singing part of this lesson and focus on the real message. *You should make your dreams come true.* Only you can do it. What is it you've always wanted to do or be and who can help you achieve that?

> "The real voyage of discovery is not in seeing new landscapes but in having new eyes." Marcel Proust

May   Week 4   Walking Tour

Pick a town, any town. Maybe the closest one to your house or one several miles away that you've always wanted to explore. Wear comfortable clothes and prepare to walk a few kilometers in shoes that will not hurt you later. Get a map or brochure if you need one. Take money for a treat.

We chose our own town, a still-almost-small place located an hour north of Palm Beach. It was settled in 1880, revitalized a hundred years later, and is now in rapid growth phase. Which means there's a lot to see when you take the time.

Like a voluptuous, partially clad bronze sculpture named Lady Abundance, whose jugs of water flow down into the fountain at her bare feet.

Like an old feed store, one of the town's first buildings, preserved at great cost and now home to the Heritage Museum.

Like a pocket park with comfortable benches, a spectacular view of the river, and two stone markers dedicated to deceased motorcycle riders by their friends. One reads: We know that in spite of the distance between us you are at peace, doing what you love the most. Riding that big highway in the sky. Ride Free."

The main downtown street has a double row of shops, art galleries, restaurants and antique stores. You can buy a 375 pound bronze lion for a mere $36,000 or inspirational crystals for $1 each; like green quartz Aventurine for career success and self-reliance or Golden Tiger Eye for integrity and willpower or rose quartz for unconditional love.

There's a new fountain in the middle of an equally new roundabout with a bronze sailfish leaping into the air amidst ocean spray. There are also sophisticated new mixed-use buildings sprouting up at half a dozen building sites.

If you're hungry, you can dine in white-cloth splendor on char-grilled steak, fingerling potatoes and a good Merlot, or stroll along the sidewalk munching garlic knots from an Italian take-out window and white pecan fudge from the candy factory.

On the night we chose to tour, bronze sculptures by Seward Johnson were on exhibit at strategic spots all over town. All looked real enough to touch: a father helping his daughter ride a bicycle in the park, a fisherman fly fishing off the RiverWalk, a violinist playing near the local theater, a woman walking a dog, a girl laying on her stomach in the grass with an open book, a man throwing a wad of paper in a garbage can.

We finished up in the city park that looks out over the river. By that time it was dark and lights were shimmering across the surface of the water. Couples and family groups strolled along, stopping to swing or take a quick trip down the slide. At the nearby recreation center, somebody was teaching a swing dance class and you could hear laughing and music through the open windows. It was as soothing as a weekend away from home.

It's always fun to see your own town like an outsider would, instead of just speeding through it on your way to someplace else.

Razors pain you;
Rivers are damp;
Acids stain you;
Drugs cause cramp.
Guns aren't lawful;
Nooses give;
Gas smells awful;
You might as well live.
• Dorothy Parker, Resume

June   Week 1   Mocha Coffee Night

Anyone in the group can call a Mocha Coffee Night any time the circumstances require one. It's meant for the big problems—the ones that drop on you so quickly you can't see any way out. Like when a badly needed raise is instantly wiped out by the need for a new drain field. Like when the divorcee across the street is moving away and you send your husband over to help her load her furniture and he decides to move with her. You get the idea.

Coffee night requires only a minimum of notice and less preparation. All you need is coffee, a comfortable place to sit a little removed from the public eye (in case you want to sob hysterically into your whipped cream) and a request for comfort. You don't even need money, your classmates will be happy to buy.

There are two mega-bookstores located near our local mall. One has squishy overstuffed chairs grouped around tables. The other has hard seated groupings and better coffee. We've spent many nights at each, sipping tall mocha lattes, working through our latest problems. We try to get the corner that has only three chairs around the coffee table so we don't weird out any unsuspecting stranger who might drop into the fourth one.

We've had a few unsuspecting fourths over the years. Once a young girl, totally engrossed in Tolstoy, fell backwards into the chair and tuned us out completely. Forty minutes later, she stood up, looking furious. "I don't know why everybody thinks he's so great," she snapped at us, "*War and Peace* sucks."

Another time a twentiesh guy sat down, listened openly to our conversation, chimed in with a few opinions of his own, and turned the discussion to nontraditional healing. He'd recently had a psychic experience and he wanted to know what we thought.

Sometimes you call a Mocha coffee night and then you don't want to go. You're too tired, the weather is too hot, you're too depressed to present yourself in public. When that happens, you have to ask yourself what will change if you don't go. Will you feel less tired, less depressed, less miserable at the end of the day if you just go to bed and stay there? And will the next day be any better? Sometimes the hardest thing about Coffee night is getting your clothes on and driving to class.

That's because you know that after you've spent twenty or thirty minutes talking about what's wrong, the next step is to list the things you're grateful for in your life. Which isn't easy when you're feeling devastated. Then you're going to have to list three good things about the person or event that's upsetting you. Also hard, particularly if it's your husband or significant other. Maybe the nicest thing you can say is 'his feet don't smell all the time.' If so, start with that. You're also going have to look at your own participation or level of involvement in the situation and leave the class with at least one constructive thing you can do about it and one positive thing you can do for yourself.

If that sounds so Pollyanna you could gag, join the crowd. We've all been there and we've all gagged. We've also learned a few things: 1) Some things just take time, time, time, to heal and you try not to die while you're putting in the time. 2) The negative impact of pain can be lightened if you can honestly see it from a different angle. And 3) It's better to keep moving while you're processing (not eating, moving). Walking, running, jogging, bicycling, water skiing, jumping out of a plane, whatever you can manage. After all, it worked for Forrest Gump.

"Resentment is anger directed at what others did or did not do." Peter McWilliams, Life 101

June   Week 2   What's In Your Head

Remember those old television ads that ran—"This is your brain—this is your brain on drugs"—accompanied by a picture of an egg frying on a sidewalk? That's kind of how your brain works on resentment. Resentment burns up love and creativity.

Below is a brain. Pretend that it's yours. Fill in the pockets with the names of people toward whom you feel resentful; people you feel have injured or offended you. Maybe your partner constantly interrupts or walks away you when you try to talk to him. Maybe your boss treats you like an idiot when you know way more than she does.

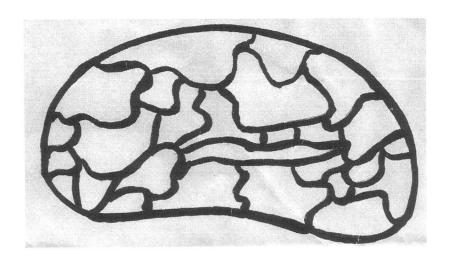

Match the size of the pocket to the amount of resentment you feel. Keep on until you run out of people. Be sure to do this as a class activity because your friends will remind you of resentments you are still holding—even when you forget.

Now transfer the names to slips of paper. Line a baking pan with foil and burn each slip of paper. Say "_____ (the person's name) I forgive you for _____ (whatever has made you angry). I forgive myself for taking it personally. I release you and I let you go." Do this for all the slips, no matter how long it takes.

Once the slips are gone and you have a squeaky clean, resentment-free brain, then what? Just let it stay empty until it fills up with new irritations? You can do that. Or you can fill those resentment-free spaces with something more positive.

Find a small glass jar and some smooth, flattish stones. You can pick them up at the beach or buy some at a dollar store. Write positive, energizing words on each stone in magic marker. Words like 'loving relationships',' harmony', 'more play', 'love', 'trust', 'prosperity', etc. Fill the jar with the stones and put it where you can look at it. Add new words or phrases as they occur to you.

Every couple of months, do the resentment exercise again. Resentment is a vexation of the spirit. Removing it as it occurs and replacing it with upbeat thoughts is good for your conscious and subconscious mind.

One last thing. If all the people you know did this exercise, how many times would your name appear on their brains?

June   Week 3   On the beach

When you first move to Florida you live at the beach. You're there Saturdays, Sundays, and weekdays after five, walking the dense wet sand of low tides, slogging through the soft sugar sand of high ones. You swim all year round, flaunt a bronzy winter tan, and carry home handfuls of striped pink and white shells. As a new Floridian, there's no such thing as a bad day at the ocean. Stormy weather is just an excuse for trudging through foamy waves and rain-splattered wind thinking profound thoughts.

But after a while other activities, more job responsibilities, too many tourists, backed up traffic, and worries about skin cancer, begin to erode away your beach time. Soon you're down to two or three times a year. Eventually you don't go at all.

One of the things we've learned in class is to utilize our resources and the ocean is too good to relegate to three visits a year. Sometimes we just walk the beach for an hour of so after work, letting the cool sea breezes blow away the stress of the day. Sometimes we spread out a blanket and picnic on subs from a nearby deli. Sometimes we have a guided meditation. The one below is a good one to tape and play back so everybody can concentrate at the same time.

Sit up straight or lie flat, fingers interlaced and eyes closed.
For a few minutes just breathe in and out, concentrating on your breath.
If your nose starts to itch, just breathe into it and let it itch.
If the sounds around you seem loud or irritating, keep breathing and let them be. Begin to breathe in and out on a count of four.
In, two, three four, out, two three, four.
Let your arms and legs relax and continue to breathe.
Begin to breathe in the things you want in your life.
Breathe in love, breathe in prosperity, breathe in good health, breathe in joy.

Breathe out on a count of four after each.

Continue to breathe in all the things you want in your life.

Breathe out the thoughts, feelings, emotions that no longer serve you.

Breathe out resentment, bitterness, misery, fear.

Release the things that no longer serve you and let them go.

Continue to breathe out the things you no longer need in your life.

Release them and let them go.

Feel your body settling into the sand.

Feel yourself grounded, connected to the earth.

Now let your mind reach out to the universe.

Let pure white light flow from the universe down through the top of your head and all through your body.

Let it flow through you, washing away the things that no longer serve you.

Let it flow through you, leaving love, prosperity, good health and joy.

Continue to breathe.

If there is something you want, state your intent now as if it were already yours.

State your intention and let it go.

(You can extend the meditation at this point, adding things you feel are important or simply stay silent for as long as you like.)

Then, continue to breathe in and out, eventually becoming more and more aware of the sounds around you, more aware of your body.

After a while, move your fingers and toes, open your eyes and stretch.

The beach is a great place to re-energize and center your self, but there are other places that work just as well. Take some time to rediscover and enjoy some of your own forgotten natural resources. Like that particular path through the woods you used to love walking. Or the bench by the lake where the ducks gather. Or that spot in your back yard, shaded by oak trees and flowering bushes, that always makes you feel so peaceful. Sitting quietly, in the midst of natural beauty, reminds you of the important things in your life and lets the unimportant things drift on to their own destination.

> "Truth is something you stumble into when you think you're going someplace else." Jerry Garcia, Grateful Dead

June   Week 4   Oxygen Bar/Art Gallery Night

This oddly combined class came about because the two places were located directly across the street from each other and forty feet from a restaurant with great mussels steamed in white wine. So the plan was, oxygen bar, gallery visit, bucket of mussels. In that order. None of us knew much about oxygen bars—except that Woody Harrellson had opened and then closed a couple of them. We pictured dark, low-ceilinged places with weirdoes hanging around to hit on you after you got your oxygen high, but we weren't sure about the high either. Did you just get sillier and sillier the more you inhaled? Did you eventually start talking like Alvin and the Chipmunks? Was it addictive and you'd soon be knocking over a 7-11 just to get an air fix? And how was breathing expensive air better than breathing free air?

Still without enlightenment, we showed up promptly at a quarter past five, ready to breathe for God and country. The small storefront shop wasn't the least bit seedy. It was painted bright beach colors and had, besides the oxygen bar, a tanning booth and a fruit smoothie bar. We checked out the toe rings and copper wind chimes, bought our plastic breathing apparatus for $2 (which were then ours to keep), and seated ourselves on stools at a navy blue glass bar with four oxygen stations. Each station had four large glass containers of different colored aromas. One end of the nose plugs went into your nostrils, the other hooked into plastic tubing attached to the containers. My station had eucalyptus, Zen (a combination of Rosemary and mint), Pumpkin Pie (cinnamon) and Revitalization (blueberry). Ronda and Cathy had aromas like Uplifting (peppermint and wintergreen), The Beach (wisteria), Purity (lemongrass) Fuzzy Naval (peach extract) and plain distilled water. There was a small switch on each container and you could breathe in one at a time, or flip all the switches at once and have an oxygen zombie if you wanted. We signed up for ten minutes each at a dollar a minute and began flipping switches. The colored water started bubbling up in the containers, we dutifully breathed, and the ten minutes went fast. Once we got used to the feeling of plastic tubes stuck up our noses, we learned a number of interesting things from the girl in charge: 1) When you normally breathe in air, you get only 21 % oxygen. At the oxygen bar you get 95%. 2) Ninety percent of your energy comes from oxygen and only 10% comes from food and water. 3) Every day you breathe 20,000 times. 4) Pure oxygen is pumped into casinos in Las Vegas to make the players feel alert and energetic.

We weren't high by the time we unhooked and crossed the street to the art gallery, but we were certainly as alert and energetic as any Vegas high roller. We also had very clean lungs.

Our plan was to walk quickly through the gallery, check out the artwork and play 'Can you find a painting you'd like to live with?' but luck intervened. We had arrived unexpectedly on opening night for an artist who'd painted hundreds of canvases depicting war and peace. We liked the paintings but found them disconcerting and hard to relate to—until a woman standing near us explained that the artist had lost her entire family in the Vietnam War and escaped with her baby strapped to her back when Saigon fell. That information made a critical difference. We began to see the huge colorful canvases in context and to feel the emotion of experiences we had never had to process.

Opening nights, like fund raisers and little theater intermissions are often a combination of bad wine, cardboard disguised as hors d'oeuvres, and poseurs holding forth on the true meaning of life. This one was absolutely different. Not only did we get to study striking paintings and hear intelligent conversation from friendly, pleasant people, we also got some remarkable cheese, sesame flat bread, and an excellent merlot. The artist spoke to the small crowd of her early background and future plans, a member of the press took pictures, and we were given a beautiful print autographed by the artist in our presence. Altogether a spectacular evening. We canceled part three of our initial plan and saved the steamed mussels for another night.

When we left the gallery, lungs still clean and alert, cultural needs satisfied, it was raining and the street made a painting of itself; smeared lights along the sidewalks, a curtain of mist hanging over the shops and restaurants beside the river, open umbrellas wet and shiny in the dark. It was the sort of painting you could live with.

Here's your assignment: First, pick an activity you've never tried. It could be a community event, a participation sport, an instructive lesson (like swing dancing or origami) or just eating at a restaurant where you're pretty sure you won't like the food.

Second, try it with the most open and positive attitude you can manage.

Third, congratulate yourself. We move beyond our unconscious safety zones one small adventure at a time.

"You are what you think." Buddha, 2500 years ago.

July   Week 1   Yoga

Yoga may be five thousand years old, but it couldn't be more present day. We had three very different experiences as we researched the perfect class: Hot Yoga, Cool Yoga, and Silly Yoga.

HOT YOGA

A hot number these days and one that lives up to its name. Hot yoga, or Bikram Yoga is meant to improve overall health and allow toxins to escape from your body during exercise. We arrived ten minutes early and joined twenty other people in a large, very warm room before a long, mirrored wall. The 100 degree dry heat came from panels in the ceiling and we worked up a sweat just unrolling our exercise mats. When the instructor arrived, we stood and began the breathing exercise, watching the mirror to make sure our stance and movements were correct. I had a hard time concentrating because I kept seeing these lumpy, fat thighs and then realizing they were mine. Unfortunately, you were directed to keep your eyes open at all times.

The instructor was great but she hated idleness. She took us through a series of twenty-six positions (each one done twice) at a steady clip. Cathy, who dislikes heat, had the most difficulty. Halfway through, nauseated and blinded by sweat, she left her mat and stumbled out into the foyer. There she collapsed on the cool stone floor and started flapping her shirt up and down. Seconds later she realized a man was sitting in the chair beside her and she was flashing him every time. He jumped up and disappeared but she was too hot to either care or stop flapping. It took fifteen minutes of cooling down before she could return and finish the session.

Ronda and I struggled on since heat doesn't make us sick, but the only thought in our minds was 'Is it over yet? Will it ever be over?'

When we reached the final segment, we got to lie on our mats and rest. We were thrilled but we rejoiced too soon. After a five second interlude, the other participants suddenly hurled themselves into a monster sit-up, exhaled in guttural, karate-like explosions of sound and began a series of eight more poses.

When it was finally over, we were pretty sure we'd lost twenty pounds between us. Our hair and clothes were as wet as if we'd been swimming and we were forced to head for the nearest outdoor pizza place to replace lost body fluids with mugs of beer and the house special.

The interesting thing was that all three of us woke the next day with more energy than we'd had in years and two of us had incredible energy all day long. The third had incredible energy until she drove her car over a cement block on the way to a meeting and had to call AAA to be helped off it. In the end, only Ronda decided to continue hot yoga. Her reason? "It feels so good when you quit."

COOL YOGA

Also known as Hatha Yoga and intended to help you balance your energy. We liked this one for a lot of reasons. For one thing, the room was cool and quiet with dimmed lights and candles glowing in every corner. That was very soothing after a long, stressful day at work. It also made us look a lot better in the huge mirror as we proceeded through child pose, corpse pose, downward dog, and cow face. The instructor had a gentle, calming voice, and endless patience. She demonstrated each position and explained how to twist yourself into it in clear, easy steps. We were encouraged to breathe properly and move slowly and carefully, holding the poses so she could check our form. I looked up at the clock at one point and was amazed to see that fifty minutes had passed instead of twenty. The last segment of the session featured a guided meditation that drained away any remaining stress and sent us out the door in a calm, self-confident mood. The morning after Hatha Yoga wasn't as high rush-high energy as the one after Bikram but the upbeat mood lasted for several days.

SILLY YOGA

Actually titled Yoga and Mat Science, which should have been a clue. This one was a trip. The setting was neither hot nor cool and there was no carpeting and no door. One long wall was mirrored but the lights were so dim you could barely see yourself in it. Only a curtain separated the yoga room from the weight lifting room. We placed our thin, very thin, towels on the oak floor and tried to tune out the grunting and groaning sounds on the other side of the curtain.

The instructor was probably thirty and she never explained a pose, what it did for your body, or how you got into it. She said things like, "When the spirit moves you, leap into warrior pose," then immediately threw herself into the posture. Sometimes she didn't mention the spirit, just leapt suddenly into a tortured looking position and shouted 'Twisted Tree.' Her favorite pose was rolling backwards around the room on a twenty-four inch exercise ball.

As a result, the three of us got a gigantic fit of giggles six minutes into the session and never got over it. After the first time, we never made eye contact again and nobody laughed out loud, but I could hear gurgling from the nearby mats and I was controlling my own growing hysteria by biting both sides of my tongue and holding my breath. Not the most peaceful way to do yoga. The rolling ball exercise did not go well. As we were bouncing around, trying to keep our balance, the woman in front of us slipped off hers and went splat on the hardwood floor in a great flailing of arms and legs. The instructor never commented or even looked up as the woman, an absolute trouper, got up and tried again.

That incident finished us. We spent the last fifteen minutes of the anything-but-serene meditation face down on the floor, tears streaming out of our eyes. From the adjoining room intermittent sounds of "Uuuuu-ungh!" and heavy weights slamming back into place overrode the instructor's direction to 'think tranquility!'

When it was finally over, we retreated to the parking lot in fairly good form but as we began debriefing, we had another laughing fit. After fifteen minutes of howling, we decided our energies needed balancing and went to find pizza and beer.

So, after intense research, our criteria for best yoga class? One that doesn't call for transfusions of hops, pepperoni and extra cheese.

See what conclusions you draw after investigating different classes and instructors. Yoga is an ancient discipline with plenty to offer the serious student.

"Thought: Why does man kill? He kills for
food. And not only for food: frequently
there must be a beverage." Woody Allen

July   Week 2   Tapas

One of the places we like meeting for class is a neighborhood tapas cafe. It's a popular spot and fabulous food is only part of its appeal. The decor is energizing, soothing, sophisticated and warm all at once with cream colored tiles on the floor, dark cream and pale cocoa walls, and architectural punctuations in a deep rich color that isn't quite red, or orange, or brown. The walls are lined with paintings and other works of art from local artists. We usually pass up a seat at the bar or at one of the tables and head for a tiny back room whose huge window overlooks the street. This room has a thick wooden table that seats eight if you're very friendly, bookshelves filled with brass candlesticks, exotic cookbooks and vases of fresh flowers. If you leave the French doors open, you can hear the flamenco guitarist playing out front. We order a glass of good wine from the eclectic wine list and decide which and how many tapas to sample.

Tapas are common fare these days, but there are still a few people around who haven't heard of them. When the cafe's two owners applied for a beer and wine license before opening, they found the city commissioners skeptical of another downtown drinking establishment. After weeks of unproductive meetings, one of the owners threw up her hands. "Okay," she said with a sigh. "Forget the beer and wine. We'll just have to settle for a tapas bar."

The lady commissioner gasped and struggled to her feet. "You can't do that," she blurted, "it's not legal!"

She thought they had said 'topless.'

For the uninitiated, tapas were invented by a Spanish taverna owner with an innovative marketing idea: serve customers arriving on horseback a glass of wine topped with a thick slice of bread while they're still in the saddle. The bread was only there to keep the flies out but the rider usually ate it anyway. In the grip of genius, the proprietor spread anchovy paste on the bread and added a tomato and—!he aqui!—the tapa was born. Also the prototype for bruschetta. And possibly the first drive in service.

We arrive by convertible rather than horseback and our small dishes of black olives baked in wine, shrimps gambas, roasted portabello, carpaccio, rosemary grilled chicken, and chips & salsa are much fancier than the fabled slab of bread. The result, however, is the same. Eat, drink, listen to music, talk. And when our husbands ask where we had class, we say, "at a topless bar."

If there's no topless or tapas bar in your area, make a list of other unique or unusual cafes or eating spots and investigate them one by one. The idea is to go where no man (sorry, woman) has gone before.

> "What we've got here is…failure to communicate."
> —Captain in Cool Hand Luke

July   Week 3   Dog Days

Sometimes our class nights evolve around a problem one of us is having and we discuss it. Sometimes we realize we all have the same problem and have no idea how to deal with it. Our rule is, no matter how small—or silly—the issue seems, if it's stressing us out, we do something about it. And that's why we talked our friend Sarah into meeting us for a cup of coffee and a discussion of animal behavior.

No, it wasn't our husbands. This time. This time it was pets—family pets and neighborhood pets. We'd tried everything we could think of—scolding, anti-chew spray, swatting with a rolled newspaper, time out, substituting toys for shoes and sunglasses, crating, kind talks, and screaming 'No, No, No!' at the top of our lungs. Nothing had worked and we needed an expert.

Sarah has a background in counseling and social work but she's a lifelong animal lover. She volunteers at the humane society, is a member of a pet therapy group, and takes her standard poodle, Laurie, to visit nursing homes. She's also taken several courses in animal communication. We waited until she got cream in her coffee and a couple of French pastries, then bombarded her with questions:

A)   Cathy's adopted shelter dog was chewing up personal belongings and chasing the cats around the house. She was reluctant to punish him because he had been abused by previous owners but he was driving everybody crazy. How did she make him stop?

B)   The neighbor's dog was peeing on Ronda's personal front doorstep two or three times a day and she was tired of scrubbing it down with clorox. How could she get him to stop?

C)   What can you do about a dog that howls and goes crazy every time it hears a threatening noise or it thunders?

Sarah knew a lot about neglected and abused dogs. She had rescued one herself—one whose kennel cough, mange, and malnutrition levels were so severe that the veterinarian recommended putting it to sleep. Instead she talked him into treating it, took it home, and nursed it for weeks. The dog had to be isolated from other pets and its skin smelled so bad she had to wear gardening gloves to pet it, but it quickly got the message that it was in a loving home and recovered completely in three months.

We learned a lot of things over coffee that day, most of it dealing with communication between people and pets. We learned that it doesn't do any good to punish animals because they can't unscramble what the punishment is for. We learned to teach your dog as you would a member of your family—showing it clearly what you want it to do instead of yelling at it. We learned not to take the animal's behavior personally—that it's usually trying to send you a message you're not understanding. We learned that dogs and cats don't have a sense of body awareness; that they don't have a clear idea where they are in relation to other animals or loud sounds which is why they sometimes go crazy during storms. We also learned that having a pet is a constant exercise in personal growth, one that teaches us to accept without expectation and to release judgment in favor of loving connection.

To the problems we had posed, we got these answers:

** Animals who urinate in inappropriate outside places have to be retrained. That means spending some time watching and waiting and in this case blowing a loud horn the minute you see them begin. After several blasts from the horn, they will get the message and move somewhere else.

** Animals who fear storms need comfort and to be provided with a space where they can feel their body in relation to their surroundings. Like curled up next to you under a comforting arm or under a small table or even in a cardboard box. When animals sense they are surrounded and safe, they will calm.

** Abused animals sometimes need more than just love and care and tolerance. A training program/book called *The Tellington Touch,* a hands-on method of healing and training animals, has proved successful in dealing with many behavior problems.

Using this 'ask the expert' approach was a great experience for us and we recommend it to your group. Check your circle of friends and acquaintances and find out who's a great resource. Invite them to come and share their information or expertise and ply them with food and drink. We all have much to offer each other; we just forget to ask.

"He who knows others is wise. He who knows himself is enlightened." Lao Tzu from the Tao

July   Week 4   Paper Dolls

What we think of ourselves—that thing called self-concept—begins the day we take our first breath. It's created and reinforced by the feedback we receive from parents, siblings, teachers, baby-sitters, neighbors and other kids; feedback that's often more critical than complimentary. As children, we must be taught how to take responsibility for mistakes. If we hear, 'You selfish brat, you little devil, where's your brain moron?' or any of the many unlovely things people say to each other when they're frustrated and angry, instead of 'What could you do next time that would be better?' we store it away deep inside. Those hidden words become potent adjectives used to describe who we believe we are.

Here's an exercise that will help reexamine some of the beliefs you hold about yourself. You've heard of working with your inner child? Well this is an exercise for your inner doll. Most of us played with paper dolls—from stylish Barbies to the primitive accordion type that have been around since paper was invented. Your adult doll will be accordion type but a little racier, a little more confident. And since a paper doll isn't truly a paper doll unless it has clothes, you'll be dressing yours in a wardrobe of your own personal characteristics. To do it, you'll need a pen, scissors, a Thesaurus, several slips of paper, and a couple of good friends.

Step 1: Copy and enlarge the paper doll sheet. (page 48) Fold it carefully. Cut where it says cut. Make the hair short or long as you prefer. Don't say it doesn't look like you because it does. Your inner doll is always slim, shapely, sexy, and cutting edge. Cut her edges out nicely.

Step 2: Lay your joined-at-the-arm dolls out flat. The one with the black-lined clothes and face is going to be the person you think you are. Turn it over and write qualities you believe you have (or have been told you have) that you would like to change. Write them clearly so you can read them later. Be honest. Here's one of our examples: selfish, impatient, quick temper, talks too much, workaholic.

Step 3: Fill out three slips of paper for each of your class mates. Write things you admire about them or think they do well, then trade slips. You now have a handful of positive feedback to share. Read your slips aloud. Do not look embarrassed, make faces or explain that they are wrong. Smile and say 'thank you' after each one.

Step 4: Write 'I am' on the back of the second doll and copy what each slip says below it. This doll is the person your friends see or think you are. It's an important one because these are admirable characteristics and most of us aren't very good at acknowledging our positive qualities.

Step 5: You now have one doll with negative and one doll with positive qualities. The last doll will integrate these and be closer to the person you really are. Look at the list of characteristics you would like to change. If 'selfish' is your first item, look it up in the Thesaurus.

Are you really all those things? Self-serving, egotistical, self-advancing, self-indulgent, self-absorbed, self-contained? Or was that just what someone told you once when you were in first grade and didn't want to share? Ask your classmates for feedback.

It may be that you're not selfish, merely private, reserved and a little shy. Write "I am" and the word that you believe is most true. Do that with every word on your list. Now look at your list of positive qualities. Write "I am" and recopy those you believe to be true on the last doll. Be honest and try to see yourselves as others do. Your personal truth is probably somewhere between the elevated opinions of your friends and the judged convictions you've held since childhood.

This exercise takes some time but it's worth it. Most of us internalize negative pronouncements and ignore positive ones. Some of the new research even indicates we're hardwired that way. Remember, it's never too late to override your programming. It is never too late to be an upbeat, confident, cutting-edge doll.

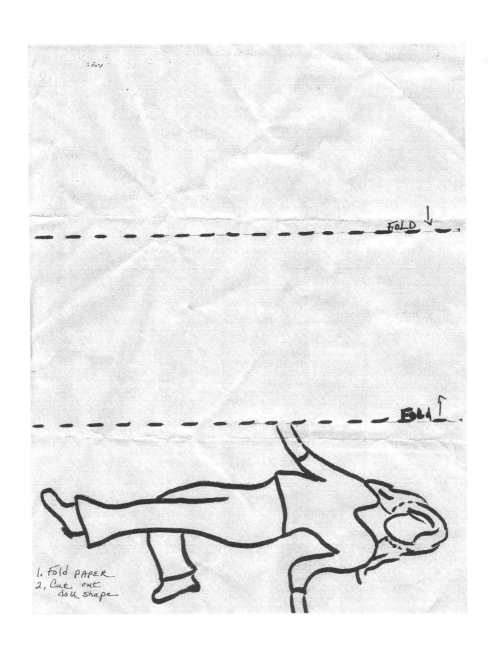

> "From the moment we cease trying to swim upstream and begin to flow with the current, something changes within us." Arthur Sokoloff

August   Week 1   Throwing Your Worries Away

We started the ceremony of throwing our troubles away by accident.

One evening we arrived at our favorite Mexican restaurant to find a thirty minute wait so we decided to spend the time walking a nearby bridge. Since the bridge opened a few years ago, it's become the equivalent of an upscale outdoor gym for walkers, runners, bicyclists and joggers. It's a gym with spectacular views.

As we trudged to the top of the sixty-five foot span, speed boats shot out from under it like toys, throwing out glittery spray as they hurried down the river. A train chugged along its own private track far below us and the setting sun turned the water shades of bronze and copper and gold. We stopped halfway up to rest and watch the water as it flowed steadily in the direction of the inlet.

"Wouldn't it be nice," somebody said," if you could just throw every problem you had over the side and let the river float them all away?"

Ronda had just returned from a weekend on Cape Cod and she'd brought back a handful of proof that the seasons do change in other spots on the globe. She reached in her jacket pocket and pulled out a handful of leaves from real up-north trees; orange, gold, red, dark and light shades of brown. "I was saving these for later," she said, "but let's do this instead. She dug through her purse for a pen and found a red magic marker. "Here."

We each got three leaves—although we thought we needed more—and we took turns writing the three things we were most worried about. The problems looked different somehow, spelled out in red ink. Smaller, and not so upsetting. We held them out over the top of the railing one at a time, let them fall out of our hands, and watched them drift slowly down, catching a current of air now and then before they disappeared into the water. And after a while we resumed walking.

They say your subconscious doesn't know what's true or not true—only what you tell it. So if you throw your worries off the bridge, does your subconscious immediately program "Problem gone! Don't worry about that anymore. Next problem?"

I don't know. I do know we walked down the bridge a lot more cheerful than we walked up it, but maybe that's because down hill is always easier.

"I've had a wonderful time but this isn't it."—Groucho Marx

August   Week 2   Water Skiing

Two of us love water skiing. One of us thinks it's about as much fun as a cold water enema. That's because one of us has weak ankles and falls over sideways every single time. However, when somebody names their pure joy night, we all do it together no matter what. That doesn't mean that if Ronda wants to parachute out of a plane we all have to take the plunge. But we do have to tag along with a positive attitude and shout 'Break a leg' or something appropriate as she flies backwards out of the cockpit.

Cathy and Ronda have their own skis and equipment so all we needed were some snacks and a boat. We rented a twenty-foot runabout at a nearby marina, packed ourselves and our cooler aboard, and pushed away from the dock and out into the river. It was after five and there weren't a lot of other people out so we flew along, wind blowing our hair in all directions, like the only craft on the water. It was the kind of evening that northerners drool over and we often forget to be grateful for; warm yellow sun side slipping down an impossibly blue sky, thick green foliage and elegant homes lining the riverbanks, cobalt blue water glinting with sunlight and tiny white caps.

While two of us took turns running the boat and spotting, the third skied expertly back and forth, flying along the tops of the waves, faces alight with—you got it—pure joy. For forty-five minutes they traded off—skiing, resting, skiing, resting, skiing again. It occurred to me that most of the world counts pure joy in seconds if they're lucky, but Ronda and Cathy had found a way to make it last three quarters of an hour.

Eventually we packed away the equipment and headed for a quiet cove. There we threw out the anchor and the one of us who does not love water skiing brought out a bottle of champagne and a basket of chicken salad sandwiches wrapped in foil and tied with ribbons. (You have a lot of free time when you're the permanent spotter.) By the time we'd wiped out our picnic supplies, it was nearing dusk and time to head back to the marina.

When I got home and my husband asked how class was and if I learned anything.

"Yep," I told him. "One, don't wear a visor when the wind's blowing. Two, never sit down on a Styrofoam cooler. And, three, second hand joy is almost as good as the real thing."

If water skiing isn't your thing either, make a list of the activities that give you pure joy and get your friends to do some of them with you. Keep adding to your list and remember: the more joy you experience, the more joy comes to you.

"Poof! Whaddaya need?" The genie from the movie Aladdin.

August   Week 3   A Carton of Wishes

Leprechauns, fairies and other fantastic folklore creatures have been granting wishes to credulous mortals for centuries, but we still love the concept today. What would you ask for if you were given three wishes—no matter how wild, outrageous, or seemingly impossible?

We like this activity because you get more than three wishes, you get an even dozen. Twelve far-out, funky, fabulous requests for you to dream up and embellish.

First do a little mental preparation. Take a piece of paper and a handful of colored pens, close your eyes, and visualize a glowing solid gold lamp. Now picture a gigantic genie smoking up out of its spout, waving a finger in your face and telling you your wishes are his command. But only if you list them in eight minutes or less and only if they're wild, crazy, and outrageous.

Got it? Now write them down as quickly as you can. Be very careful <u>not</u> to put down things you want other people to do to make you happy. For example:

1.   I want my son to marry somebody who will fit into the family instead of that girl who bosses him around.

2.   I want my boyfriend to stop paying attention to other women.

3.   I want my boss to like me better than his secretary who spends all day talking on the phone to friends when he's not around.

These wishes are out of your control and in this exercise your wishes are just for *you*.

Can you re-frame the above to fit within your sphere of influence? Try again, how about:

1.   I want a happy family who spends time together talking and sharing.

2. I want a loving relationship with a partner I care about.

3. I want to be a success at a job I like.

That's better, right? Well, marginally. We're talking boring here and the genie's talking wild, crazy, out of the box, thinking. Let's rewrite them in outrageous-ese.

1. I want a huge, supportive, wildly successful family who spends hours around the dinner table talking and laughing and eating and drinking.

2. I want a drop-dead, rich hunky partner/husband who worships the ground I walk on and flies me to France for dinner when I don't feel like cooking.

3. I want to run my own travel consulting business and plan large parties for corporations in Bora Bora and London and Marrakech.

Now that you've got the idea, go for it. Here are a few more for inspiration.

1. I want to spend a month in Tuscany learning to cook northern Italian food.

2. I want to moonlight as a Victoria's Secret model.

3. I want to own a New England bed and breakfast with ten luxury cottages, a full spa, and a staff of masseurs, maids, chefs, and gardeners.

4. I want to climb Mount Everest with a gorgeous (and tall) Sherpa guide

There's nothing too wild or impossible to go on your list. Write down everything you've ever wanted but never expected to have. When you're finished, place a star by the one that's most important at the moment and put the list in a dream jar or secret box or a private drawer. Take it out periodically, read it, and imprint this quotation from Thoreau in your brain:

"If one advances confidently in the direction of his dreams, and endeavors to live the life which he has imagined, he will meet with a success unimagined in common hours."

August   Week 4   Thrift Store Shopping

Twice a year we shift our class night to a Saturday and do a pub crawl through the thrift shops. We go high end to low end and everything in between, fancy consignment stores, flea markets, charity shops and auction houses. Sometimes we have a specific purchase in mind, sometimes we're just looking for inspiration. We do it right; wear our running shoes, carry bottles of water so we don't pass out if it's a warm day, and prepare to negotiate—not haggle.

We've found some interesting offbeat pieces; a headboard carved like the sun's rays, a green antique punchbowl, and a bench made out of an ox yoke, but the most fun was the day we decided to put together at least one complete outfit apiece, fully accessorized, for forty dollars or less.

The consignment shop we chose turned out to be the most organized used-clothing store on earth. Everything—dresses, blouses, skirts, jackets, shorts, slacks, shoes, bags, hats, scarves, and jewelry were arranged on easily accessible racks by size and color. Blues, reds, golds, browns, greens, whites, blacks, pinks. Everything was clean and pressed, all of it high quality, and some of it new.

The lady who ran the consignment store was full of ideas on adapting and accessorizing and she told the flat, unvarnished, sometimes ugly truth about how you looked in your choices. We tried on dresses, tops, bottoms, shoes, etc. and two hours later we had put together these outfits:

Cathy: classic knee-length little black dress
          black strappy heels
          silver bow earrings and pin
          black dressy sweater
          black clutch

Ronda: shiny silver and gray tiny flowered skirt
         black velvet tank with square diamante shoulder fasteners
         silver strapped heels
         gray satin evening purse with a long silver chain
         rhinestone chain earrings.

Sandy: sequined bronze open backed tank
         narrow legged beige jeans
         bronze, gold and brown backless heels
         faux lizard shoulder bag
         giant gold drop earrings

Each outfit fell well under the forty dollar limit and we left the store feeling luxurious, creative and thrifty. One week later, on class night, we dressed in our put-together outfits and met for dinner to celebrate our fashion savvy. We looked fabulous.

> "What is important is to keep learning, to enjoy challenge, and to tolerate ambiguity. In the end there are no certain answers."
> Martina Horner, President of Radcliffe College

September/October   Weeks 1-8   Study Nights

We schedule sixteen study nights a year, eight in the spring (March and April) and eight in the fall (September and October). During those weeks we work our way through books and workbooks we've discovered or that have been recommended by friends. We take turns presenting lessons and activities and focus on who we are (and have become) and how we function in our world.

It's impossible to list all the things each of us has learned over the last few years. And even though we've worked together and shared experiences, our learning as been as diverse as the people we are. Here are some comments we'd like to share with you.

Cathy: Study nights were difficult for me at first. I wasn't comfortable with self-reflection. I had a tendency to focus mostly on outward things and the inner me ended up pretty much unexplored. I wasn't sure what I liked, disliked, or what my opinions were in general. My friends, on the other hand, were pros at processing their thoughts. They had been soul searching for a few years before I became part of the group. This left me some nights feeling emotionally inadequate. My angelic classmates, Sandy and Ronda, however encouraged me and became my guides without intellectual conceits. Their patience, prodding and prime examples put me on the path to introspection. The more exposure and experience I gained at the art of self-analysis, the clearer my thoughts and desires became. Some nights I was traveling in the speed lane and accelerated through what would have taken years of therapy—unraveling my emotionally bruised childhood.

I remember a particular class in which I made substantial growth. Our group had a discussion on healing our inner child. Later that night I awoke, crouched in the fetal position, holding a child and crying. I wrapped my arms around that little six year old girl, rocked and reassured her that it would be all right. As I drifted

57

off to sleep, I remembered some of my childhood fears. I recalled as a toddler how I'd wake up in the middle of the night and slip into my mother's bed to sleep there til morning. She slept alone since the death of my dad. He died several months before I was born. She didn't seem to mind sharing the bed with me or maybe she was too exhausted rearing three toddlers alone and didn't have the energy it took to place me back in my own bed. This six year habit didn't fare well when she remarried. I soon found out that there was no room in their bed for me.

When I tried to invade their room in the wee hours I was taken back to my own bed. I felt as though my new stepfather was stealing my mother's love from me. I remembered many nights of sneaking under their bed just to be close to her. One night my hair got stuck in the exposed box springs and I woke up screaming. After that their bedroom door was shut and locked in the evenings. I still get teary eyed when I think about how that little girl felt. Healing those emotional bruises will take time but at least I know why those areas of my life became tender.

One of the activities I liked best during study nights was writing a letter describing what you projected or wished would occur in your life for the coming year. The letter was not to be opened for one full year and on that anniversary you read what was so important to you a year ago. I still remember how my son was such a worry to me. He was in his junior year in high school. He had just left my home to live with his dad. His grades were suffering, drugs were a great influence, and I had no control over my seventeen year old child. The ordeal was heavy on my heart for months. My letter, when I opened it a year later, told of the pride I felt when my son graduated from high school. It described the graduation celebration that took place, who attended, and how much Eric loved the car he had earned for graduating with honors. The letter also contained blurbs about my husband's health, retirement, a cabin in the mountains, growth of friendships, and enjoyment of my job, but the major focus was my son. Unbelievably, 90% of the wishes in the letter had come true

Ronda: Our weekly class meetings have changed my life. I am not the person I was six years ago, I am stronger and more at peace. I have learned that my 'victim mentality' did not serve me well. I have learned that my realm of control is limited and that I cannot make or wish those around me to fit my expectations. Rather, I can put my energy towards evolving into the person I want to be.

I grew up as a 'pleasing child' who more easily tuned into others than to myself. I valued what they thought and measured my own worth by how they treated me. As a result, it seemed I had mastered the keys to a successful life.

Our class gave me the safety and acceptance to explore places in myself that were far from perfect. Scary places. Ugly places. Unworthy places. The more I opened up, the more I felt the genuine love of my friends. I had lived my whole life motivated by the fear of rejection but with these friends I felt accepted regardless of what unpleasant part of me I shared.

One class night we were listing (1) ten positive attributes that described us, then (2) ten words that meant the opposite'—things we believed we were <u>not</u>, and finally (3) ten synonyms that were the flip side of positive, yet were inoffensive enough for us to accept as part of ourselves. It was a challenging exercise: "I am <u>nice</u>—I am not <u>mean</u>—but I am <u>self absorbed</u>. The point was to illuminate the dark and light in each of us. This was particularly eye opening for me as I had practiced all my life to hide my dark side from others. As we shared our descriptions it became steadily more comfortable to be defined by (3), yet I shuddered at the thought I might also be the ugly words in (2). Then I realized that (2) included the very words I accused my husband of being. My pattern became quickly clear. When my husband wasn't 'nice,' in my opinion, I promptly deemed him 'mean' without any allowance for other possibilities. Was he really mean when he didn't respond to me or our kids with a gentle loving tone? Or was he simply tired or preoccupied? Wow! If I could learn to accept—no embrace—the less desirable parts of me, then I could learn to reprocess less desirable behaviors in my husband and in everyone else too.

I frequently return to this activity to mentally change my old ways. If someone at the store steps ahead of me in line I may think 'How rude.' then 'no, maybe self absorbed, maybe tired, stressed, grieving?' If I make a mistake, I catch my thought and move it from 'How stupid of me' to "I need to slow down and concentrate.' I have a long way to go but I am learning to love myself. And as I drop judgments of myself I discontinue the pattern of judging others.

Because of the work I've done in class, I am a better wife. I appreciate my husband as a quality person with flaws of his own and no longer expect him to be my savior or the knight in shining armor who rescues me from myself and others. The truer I become, the closer my husband draws to me. My former neediness only pushed him away. I am also a better parent. I am consistently given opportunities to let go of the fear of what other people think and accept my grown teen-aged children, mistakes and all. Each of my children is a unique creation. None of them are me nor are they necessarily a reflection of me. I support them and love them. I am growing up.

Sandy: All my life I felt like the late bloomer in my group—the really, really late one. Everyone else seemed to understand how life worked: find a boyfriend, date heavily, get married, have children (when I grew up that was the order). But while my friends were delivering offspring to preschool and going to little league games and paying off mortgages I was still backpacking around Europe, still managing a guest house in New England summers, still having coke and potato chips for breakfast if the spirit moved me. I had a good job as a speech therapist but I moved around—teaching in Iowa, Rhode Island, Colorado, Florida. I liked meeting new people and seeing new places but mostly I didn't want to end up like so many of the people I knew. To me they seemed tired, tied down, bored out of their gourds, living only through their children.

Being responsible only for yourself is a mixed blessing. On one hand you get to do exactly as you like. On the other you're often lonely and holidays can be real downers. Valentine's Day can be particularly bad for your self concept: Doesn't somebody love you madly? Guess not. Nobody brought flowers or candy. Loser!

You also miss a critical growing-up rite of passage—marriage—and that puts you outside a huge segment of the mainstream. There are worse things of course, like a friend of mine who married three times and, in her words, rited and rited and rited until she got it wrong. But still.

I didn't get married until I was way past the date you have more chance of being maimed by a terrorist than walking down the aisle. My husband was a handsome, conservative man who didn't know what a crystal healer was and was never going to wake up Tuesday morning and decide to move to the Galapagos. He preferred prime rib and mashed potatoes to stuffed portabellos and Vietnamese shrimp rolls, balanced his check book every month, organized the clothes in his closet, and actually knew where the warranty for the microwave was. I overlooked his shortcomings and married him anyway. Only love—true love—can make a former backpacker settle down to suburban living and that was when my real personal work began. All my judgments, of self and others, began to surface. I was not the laid back, easy going person I thought; I was a longtime, practiced, control freak.

My view of marriage was also exceedingly unrealistic. Life was, shock and dismay, not going to be two people working their way through problems with total understanding and smiling agreement. It wasn't going to be nonstop romantic dinners and love songs either.

I finally saw that married life was going to be a compromise, not a word in my personal dictionary, and it was a shock when our first Christmas tree looked like an exercise in schizophrenia. Half of it was decorated in white lights with angel hair and all white ornaments—the other half was done up in red and green lights, silver tinsel, and multicolored glass balls.

I began to realize that the love of my life was not going to fulfill all my needs; worse yet, he wasn't going to read my mind to figure out what they were.

The value of study nights for me has been learning not to shift the responsibility for my happiness to my husband; learning to stop reading meaning into actions that are his alone; learning that when I'm bored, it's up to me to get UNbored instead of expecting him to entertain me; learning that hopping on a plane for somewhere else is not an option when we have serious disagreements that neither will back down on; and learning that, as partners, you ultimately improve a relationship because you improve your half of it.

November   Week 1   Zumba

The problem with exercise is, that no matter how good it is for you, it's only fun the first ten minutes. In our search for the perfect fitness class—perfect meaning one you will continue to do after the first two sessions—we've tried walking, jogging, Tai-Bo, spinning, step aerobics, fencing, yoga, pilates and something called Boot Camp. All were beneficial, some were intriguing, and some were just plain painful. But Zumba was the only one that was fun every single time.

Zumba is a kind of dance-aerobics that's part salsa, flamenco, calypso, samba, tango, merengue, conga, cha cha and God knows what else. It was invented by a fitness instructor in Columbia who forgot the exercise tapes for his early morning aerobics class and had to substitute salsa tapes instead. When he adjusted the beat to fit the music and inserted dance steps, he became the instant father of an international exercise craze.

Zumba's sound is fast, loud, and exhilarating, the steps are easy to follow, and the instructions are simple: just dance non-stop for forty-five minutes and shake everything that isn't fastened down. Oh yeah, you have to shout 'Caramba!' and 'Arriba!' and 'Ride 'em cowboy' every now and then too.

We thought Zumba was more like a party—a wild Brazilian party—than a workout and the aftermath was better too. Instead of dragging out to the car exhausted, achy and dehydrated, we left laughing, energetic and feeling ten years younger than when we arrived. Okay, maybe six years younger.

If they don't do Zumba in Rio at Carnival they ought to. It's better than champagne, better than a shopping spree, better than an hour of therapy. And if you can schedule your Zumba session for first thing in the morning, you'll move to a Latin beat all day long.

Have any Zumba classes or something equally zesty in your area?Advanced Kung fu? Australian kick boxing? Check out all the wild things and give them a try. Don't give up until you'll find something you love.

> **"In all things of nature there is something marvelous."** Aristotle 384—322 BC

November   Week 2   Playing Outside

Remember when your mom used to make you turn off the TV and go outside to ride your bike? There's still nothing like a long bike ride in the fresh air for clearing out mental cobwebs and burning off a couple of hundred calories, but we like having a destination rather than simply coasting around dodging traffic. So we often pedal in the direction of a recently opened riverside park. This park is fun because it's always full of people. Families picnic in the shelters or under the shade trees, children run in and out of the mosaic-design interactive pool, people walk their dogs along the paved walkways and fish off the half mile long fishing pier. There's a two story multipurpose building that hosts Girl Scout meetings, karate classes, and the occasional wedding but it also has rocking chairs on the porch so if you're not feeling energetic you can just sit and watch the boats go by.

Even in the heat of summer this sixty-three acre, pond-filled park exudes a kind of cool, soothing, work-in-progress energy. An on-site building, once a chapel, will soon become a children's museum with a two-story hands-on Spanish treasure ship, an Indian encampment, and a simulated archaeological dig. A thirties mansion that sits atop a 4,000 year old Indian burial ground is being renovated for community activities. And eventually there will be a butterfly garden, an amphitheater, and stage, and….

There are dozens of parks around that go unused and unnoticed; tiny pocket parks, sports parks, parks with bird sanctuaries, parks for surfing or hiking or back packing or canoeing or in-line skating. Get out your helmet, pump up those tires and go explore one. Then you can tell your kids with a perfectly clear conscience, to turn off the video games and go out to play.

November   Week 3   Paint Night

Most of us like to paint but we rarely take time to do it. It isn't just the painting itself—it's more like needing a color fix every once in a while, and then realizing your paint tubes are twenty years old, canvas is expensive, and you weren't that good at it anyway. Remember when the art teacher tried to teach you about perspective?

We think people should paint. All people. And they don't have to invest in ten dollar brushes or costly acrylics or huge canvases either. The Highwaymen, Florida's famous folk-art painters, worked on roofing board, paneling and just about every other surface available. Michaelangelo painted ceilings. And Picasso once created a complete work of art on the dusty side of a journalist's car.

We treated ourselves to a luxurious paint night recently but instead of using stretched canvas, we painted on pieces of plywood Ronda's husband had cut to board up their house for hurricanes. (Before you gasp in horror, it was his idea.) We collected brushes and rollers, old cans of paint and even made a trip to the do-it-yourself stores for 'oops' paint. Oops paint is paint that's been mixed in error, resulting in strange, wild colors that nobody wants to put on their walls. We bought orangey-red, pale blue, dust blue, daffodil, sand beige, mimosa pink and something called navy green.

We put on our painting clothes, smoothed out a tarp in the garage, and began to create on smooth clean pieces of plywood. Our styles were meticulous, diverse, and in my case nonexistent. We had a great time. Neighbors came walking by and stopped to look and make comments. A neighborhood dog ran through the garage and across the length of the orange and purple Jackson Pollock painting Cathy was doing. Then he ran back again and shot out into the street. He left painty tracks all the way out of the garage but it didn't change the painting much.

When we finished we had a semi-Pollock, a Mondrian, some tall palm trees, a field of wildly colored flowers, a French hotel and one intriguing brown/khaki surface (too much mixing).

Our husbands had kidded us all week about art class and suggested we do nude self portraits, so just before we cleaned our brushes we leaned one narrow six foot tall strip of plywood upright and painted a Picasso style nude on it. She had one black thick-lashed eye, a giant red mouth, two small round pink boobs, a curved hip, one hand, and a foot with toenail polish. Oh yes, and a diamond in her belly button. We each took turns adding parts and signed our initials in the right hand corner.

When the hurricanes came, and they did—four times—our Picasso nude covered the window in Ronda's foyer. (Who says form doesn't follow function?) She and her husband laughed every time they walked by it. Their teenaged son was appalled.

For your own color-fix-class night, choose surfaces to paint on, colors to paint with, and a place to create. Then go wild.

> **"I like being married. It's so great to find that one special person you want to annoy for the rest of your life." Rita Rudner**

November   Week 4   Partner Appreciation

There is one unalterable law of the universe when it comes to relationships: No matter how exciting, romantic, fascinating, and just plain hot your partner is, the time will come when you find yourself mentally picking out curtains for your brand new single person, stress-free, him-free apartment. We call that F.U. Syndrome—as in Fed Up. Ha, ha fooled you.

To avoid getting to that point, we regularly practice a little routine relationship management. Relationships, like cars, don't just take care of themselves, although you sometimes coast along for weeks and months assuming the fuel pump is fine. But neglecting your Toyota when you're tired or too busy just results in lack of transportation. Neglecting your partner means you lose that special feeling of connection that brought you together in the first place. Relationship maintenance begins in your own head, with your own feelings, beliefs, expectations, and disappointments. You can't change those in someone else, only deal with your own. We start by writing a letter to our partners:

Date: _____

Dear _____

Lately I've been too _____ tired, overworked, sick, bummed, aggravated, menopausal, stressed-out (pick any or all of the above) to pay attention or spend quality time with you. First, I appreciate the way you always _____ _____ (you're on your own here. If you can, list several things he does that you like.) but you drive me crazy when you _____ _____ (try to keep it to one page.)

I first fell in love with you because you _____
and I still love it when you _____.
I love your _____. (You can be
as explicit as you want here; you do not have to share.) I'm grateful that you
_____   _____.   Thank   you   for
_____. My wish for us is that we_____

_____

    Love, _____ (sign your name)

    Now write your partner's name and your name on the following lines and list
at least ten good qualities under each. _____   _____

    Now fold up the letter and put it away. This one is just for you. Reread it the
next time you feel less than grateful your partner is in your life.

    And if you come home from class, feeling kind and loving and excited to see
him and he's watching football, doesn't want to be interrupted and is considerably
crabbier than when you left the house, don't get mad and flush that carefully
crafted epistle. Be pleasant, go do something nice for yourself and practice being
not-needy. The letter is a powerful tool. Give it time to do its work.

"The best and safest of things is to keep a balance in your life, acknowledge the great powers around us and in us. If you can do that, and live that way, you are really a wise man." Euripides 484-406 BC

December   Week 1   Balancing Your Life

You read a lot about living a balanced life and it sounds like a good idea, but how do you do it? Can you achieve balance when you spend a third of the day sleeping and over a third getting to, being at, and returning from work? When you have less than seven hours a day to fit in the following and more?

Cleaning house

Personal care

Exercise

Hobbies

Time with your partner

Time with your children

Spiritual time

Preparing and eating meals

Laundry

Reading (newspaper, magazine, book)

Paying bills

Decorating the house

Doctor, dental, hair appointments

Supervising homework

Chauffeuring children to activities

_____

_____

Before you get really depressed, remember: balancing your life isn't about getting through the checklist; it's about balancing your energies. Lack of sleep, lack of exercise, lack of quiet time and junk food nutrition all put you out of whack. When you're out of balance, even minor stress can turn you into a screaming meemie.

Here are a few suggestions for your mental, physical, spiritual, and emotional well-being.

Mental

1. Add to or subtract from the list above until it reflects your priorities. Put a star by ones you can afford to pay someone else to do. Check the ones you can get help with—from your husband, children, neighbors or relatives.

2. Buy a calendar, put it next to your telephone and write every appointment, meeting and scheduled activity on it. Put a smaller calendar in your purse and do the same thing. Compare the calendars every few days. (If you're a techno kind of gal, do it on computer or palm pilot.)

3. Every Sunday before you go to bed make a hit list, AKA a to-do list for the following week. Check off the items as you do them.

Physical

1. Get some exercise <u>every day</u>. Just 15 minutes worth if that's all you have time for but get it. Put it on your Sunday checklist. Try to work up to 30 minutes three times a week.

2. Eat at least one fresh vegetable and one fresh fruit <u>every day</u>. Eat one less chocolate, or potato chip, drink one less glass of soda. Drink some water—even if you hate it.

3. Make sure you get the sleep you need <u>every night.</u> Sleep keeps you sane.

Spiritual

1. Put church or group or whatever you do for your soul on your list and do it.

2. Go to bed three minutes early and do a meditation <u>every night</u>. Visualize yourself beautiful, intelligent, healthy, strong, loving and kind. Say 'There is time and space for everything I want to do" over and over until you go to sleep.

3. Keep a running gratitude list on your refrigerator. Add something every day that you're grateful for. Particularly when you're looking for a snack.

Emotional

1. Do something nice for yourself every day. Do your nails, do the crossword, read a chapter of a book you like, drink a cup of tea, stand out in the yard and stare at a tree.

2. Do something fun with your family at least once a week. Watch a movie with your partner, bake cookies with your children, take everybody to the beach, play a board game or touch football.

3. Talk to a friend when you're feeling overwhelmed—somebody who listens, doesn't tell you what to do, and understand you need to vent without prejudice. Do the same for her.

When you have more time, you can invent a cure for AIDS, start your own Fortune 500 Company, and save the whales. For now, concentrate on balancing your life by attending to the small details. They make all the difference and, lucky for us, they're within our sphere of influence.

"…. pleasures of the winter kitchen. The bubble-bubble
of soups and broths, the simmer of the stock-pot."
Susan Hill, <u>Through the Kitchen Window</u>

December   Week 2   Lobster Bisque & Goals

Florida can get cold in December, at least cold by our standards. When the temperature drops to fifty or less, it's a perfect time to don sweaters or jackets and head to an ocean side restaurant for lobster bisque and a glass of wine. We skip the outside deck and sit inside at a table between the bar and the exotic fish tank. From there we still have a clear view of waves rolling in but none of the shivering.

When the bisque is completely gone and the hot crusty bread with butter a memory, we order coffee, take out pens and paper and write our history of the year to come. We do it in reverse, listing the events we hope will occur as if they had already happened. Our lists aren't novel length; just one or two pages—and we don't share or read them aloud.

When we've finished, we check them over to make sure we really want all those things, then roll them up, slide them into a small mailing tube and tape the tube shut. On the outside we write 'To Be Opened' and the date of the following year and one of us takes it home and puts it on a closet shelf. Then we get out the tube we wrote the previous year to see if we attained our goals.

One amazing thing is that you often forget some of the things you listed, those things that were so important to you a year earlier. A more amazing thing is that most of the dreams, wishes and hopes you wrote down did come true, and in just the way you envisioned them.

> "No matter how slow the film, spirit always
> stands still for the photographer it has chosen."
> • Minor White, More Quotations From (God)

December   Week 3   The Best Years of Our Lives

This lesson takes a little pre-class homework, but only a little. Sort back through your old pictures, especially the ones that have been in the box under your bed for the past fifteen years, and pick several shots of yourself that you like. Choose the ones that make you smile as soon as you see them. Some will be rites of passage photos: birth, first year of kindergarten, prom, high school graduation, marriage, birth of children, and so on. Some will be pictures of your 'bests.' Like the year you worked at the Jersey shore selling hot dogs or the summer you lived in a teepee until it got so cold your washcloth froze to the ground or the time you caught the four pound fish right in front of your father who's an award winning fisherman. Maybe there's one of the year you did the archeological dig in Wales, or one of you and the first new car you ever bought with your own money or a group pic of the high school play—the one where you got a standing ovation.

Sort them all out and put them in chronological order by age, in a small photograph book. Attach one to each page and write a short paragraph that describes it. This is your personal pictorial biography, your visual record of bests; successes and passages. Leave a few blank pages for any pictures you might have overlooked and for the new 'bests' that are to come.

On the last pages of the book list other great things you accomplished when there was no photographer present. Share some of your accomplishments with your group. At home, put the book within easy reach and look through it whenever you need to remind yourself of the amazing life you're living.

December   Week 4   Celebrating Our Growth

Every year around Christmas time, we have a celebration and invite friends to join us for dinner. We ask them to bring themselves and a wrapped book or treasure that they've loved but are now ready to pass along.

We get out the antique red dishes and thin wine glasses and white candles, decorate the table with fresh smelling evergreens, and cook the fabulous foods we love; miniature baked onion soups, spinach and feta cheese pizza, a roasted vegetable lasagna with tomato garlic coulis, chicken with mushrooms and olives, berry-berry pie, a chocolate pudding torte with chocolate leaves on top. We wear our most glittery outfits and eat out on the patio, Tuscan style, if it's warm enough.

When the dishes are cleared we pass out glittery gold stars—blank on one side—and write the answer to 'What keeps your light bright?' on the back. Then we put them in a basket, shake them up, and draw them out again. We take turns reading them aloud and take the one we read home to hang on our tree. It doesn't matter if we draw one we didn't actually write. It's an exercise in sharing our good, in sharing our light, and everyone always seems to get the perfect one.

Afterwards we exchange the treasures we brought over cups of coffee or tea and each person gets a chance—if she wants it—to recount the highlights of her year and her plans for the year to come.

We finish the evening with a group affirmation and we keep saying it until we believe it: "I am a powerful, intelligent, loving, beautiful, creative, woman in charge of my own life and I can handle it."

> "The world is round and the place which
> may seem like the end may also be the
> beginning." Ivy Baker Priest, 1958

The End

Thanks for coming with us on this twelve month personal journey. Our intent was to inspire you and your friends to form a group of your own, to provide a format for doing it, and to give you humorous and practical suggestions for making it work. We live in a constant state of mental, physical, emotional and spiritual evolution and how we evolve is up to us. We may begin our journey by shedding anguished tears over lost opportunities, youthful mistakes, and disastrous choices. The trick is to move beyond pain and self blame. To forgive ourselves and put our mistakes in perspective. To be able, eventually, to laugh—okay, smile at least—at where we've been and to cut ourselves some slack as we focus on where we're going. Aunt Lili figured that out—by herself—many years ago but I think she'd have preferred a group of like-minded women to listen, give her feedback, and support her in the pursuit of her dreams. After all, cowboys are entertaining, but girlfriends keep you sane.

Made in the USA